Book of Terror
SERIAL KILLERS
TRIVIA

Crook Crook

Copyright©2022
ALL RIGHTS RESERVED

INTRODUCTION

For the true crime-obsessed, *Book of Terror: Serial Killer Trivia* will bring you closer to the world of serial killers. We will explore the minds of those who committed horrendous crimes, trying to figure out the motives behind their acts of evil.

Whether you want to learn about serial killers to understand the dark side of human nature, or curiosity is just too hard to resist, this book offers diverse and intriguing perspectives on 20 of history's most notorious murderers. Even if you think you already know the full story, reading the entire book can help you better understand the circumstances of these criminals and their victims' tragic fates.

TABLE of CONTENTS

WHAT ARE SERIAL KILLERS?

There has been considerable debate among criminologists about the proper definition of serial murder. The term serial murder was popularized in the 1970s by Robert Ressler, an investigator with the Behavioral Science Unit of the U.S. Federal Bureau of Investigation (FBI). The FBI originally defined serial murder as involving at least four events that take place at different locations and are separated by a cooling-off period.

In most definitions now, however, the number of events has been reduced, and even the FBI lowered the number of events to three in the 1990s. The FBI's definition has been faulted because it excludes individuals who commit two murders and are arrested before they can commit more and individuals who commit most of their murders in a single location.

Such criticisms have led many scholars worldwide to adopt the definition put forward by the National Institute of Justice, an agency of the U.S. Department of Justice, according to which serial murder involves at least two different murders that occur "over a period of time ranging from hours to years."

=>>> The different discussion groups agreed on a number of similar factors to be included in a definition.

These included:

- one or more offenders
- two or more murdered victims
- incidents should be occurring in separate events, at different times
- the time period between murders separates serial murder from mass murder

In combining the various ideas, the definition was crafted:

Serial Killer: The unlawful killing of two or more victims by the same offender(s), in separate events.

How are serial killers different from mass murderers?

The time period between murders separates serial murder from mass murder. Generally, mass murder was described as several murders occurring during the same incident, with no distinctive time period between the murders. These events typically involved a single location, where the killer murdered several victims in an ongoing incident.

Lack of Empathy

One of the most common characteristics of serial killers is a lack of emotional depth. In particular, empathy. This trait is common in both sociopaths and psychopaths, and therefore present in the majority of serial killers. However, this isn't to say that a serial killer will lack empathy for absolutely everything and everyone.

A serial killer can show empathy towards another human being, although that human being rarely becomes one of their victims. Several studies have shown that serial killers will be fully aware of their victim's distress, they just won't feel it themselves. For example, there have been several serial killers throughout the years who adored their pets. Dennis Nilsen, John Wayne Gacy, and Harold Shipman were all dog lovers. The most bizarre entry in this category may be Jeffrey Dahmer, who happily decapitated local dogs he found in his street, yet would never hurt his spaniel.

Lack of Remorse

This goes hand-in-hand with the entry above. Once again, serial killers will rarely feel remorse for their crimes.

Many serial killers have vocally opposed this trait, with some claiming that they'd learned to feel remorse after a significant time has passed since their crimes. Some people believe this is no more than a manipulation tactic, and given that many serial killers are skilled at concealing their true intentions, it's impossible to know the truth.

Psychologists and researchers into the criminal mind claim that on a whole, serial killers do not feel remorse, and all other claims are made for their benefit. There may be exceptions, but these instances are very rare (and possibly another form of manipulation).

Grandiosity

Grandiosity also goes hand-in-hand with their inflated self-perception – or narcissism. Most serial killers are obsessed with how they're perceived by the press, police, and the general public, which is why they'll sometimes attempt to control the narratives of their stories.

Many aren't afraid to brag publicly about their crimes if they believe it will give them the attention they crave.

Serial killers often confess once caught to ensure that their names are attached to the atrocities that they have committed. What's important to them is that their name is etched in true crime lore.

Narcissism

Most serial killers love to boast of their accomplishments. A lot of them see themselves as above the law and smarter than everyone else. For example, Jack the Ripper, the Zodiac Killer, or BTK taunted police and the press with letters and messages. As recently as 2009 we've seen the Long Island Serial Killer taunt his victim's family via phone call. For the serial killer, this is a way of reliving their crimes and prolonging the pain they caused, as well as displaying their guile and prowess at evading capture.

Superficial Charm

Not all killers may exhibit antisocial behavior. Many serial killers have been described as charming and charismatic.

Charisma and charm go hand-in-hand with manipulation, and serial killers know this. They know that charming someone will naturally make the other person feel more at ease in their presence and thus become more vulnerable. We've all heard the stories about famous serial killer Ted Bundy being the ultimate charmer, but it's not just about looks or attraction.

Charm and charisma can come in many varieties. While Charles Manson might not have been physically appealing, he had enough charisma to convince a whole group of people to kill for him. Likewise, John Wayne Gacy was not appealing to the eye either, but he was likable and pleasant enough to convince young boys to come back with him to his home.

With this being said, some serial killers suffer from awful social skills and aren't able to interact with their victims and gain their trust through charm or charisma at all. These are the low IQ, sociopathic killers who blitz-attack their victims to gain an immediate advantage (Peter Sutcliffe, Jeffrey Dahmer, Ed Gein).

Manipulation

Once the serial killers have gained the victim's trust, it makes it easier for them to manipulate their potential victims into vulnerable situations that they might not have allowed themselves to be drawn into in normal circumstances.

For example, Dean Corll murdered at least 28 young boys in

the early 1970s after luring them to his home where he tortured, raped, and killed them.

However, it wasn't just Corll's manipulation skills that he applied to his victims, he also applied them to two accomplices who helped source the victims for him.

Addictive Personality

Addiction is defined as the repetition of a behavior despite its harmful consequences. Many serial killers exhibit addictive tendencies outside of murder. Jeffrey Dahmer, Ted Bundy, and Dean Corll were all heavy drinkers, and some killers have even claimed that they were addicted to serial murder.

The Macdonald Triad

Experts believe that The Macdonald Triad posits three specific behaviors in children which suggest a person may become violent as an adult: bed-wetting, fire starting, and childhood abuse towards animals.

The belief is that these three traits display a lack of self-control and a lack of empathy, two things that contribute to the makeup of a homicidal adult. As we've seen from many serial killers (Jeffrey Dahmer, Edmund Kemper, John Wayne Gacy, Ted Bundy), animal cruelty is a staple of their childhood. Arson and bed-wetting are a little harder to clarify since many instances of this may have gone unrecorded. In recent years, the Macdonald Triad has become less associated with potential serial killers and more associated with parental abuse and psychological defects. However, this kind of upbringing can greatly attribute to the making of a serial killer.

Lust for Power

Many serial killers desire power and dominance, either because it provides a sexual thrill or because they lack these attributes in other areas of life. While individual motivations for murder will vary, a desire for power is one of the most common, at least amongst sexually-motivated serial killers. These offenders enjoy the act of murder because it gives them control over life and death, which to them is the ultimate satisfaction. Power play can also be a factor after a killer is caught.

For example, Moors Murderer Ian Brady refused to reveal the burial location of his final victim as a way to assert his power over police, the victim's family and the general public.

Sensation-Seeking

Imagine going through life without ever feeling any kind of emotion. Imagine looking at your partner or your children and feeling nothing whatsoever. No love, just indifference. This is how some serial killers live their lives.

Sensation-seeking is the act of engaging in reckless and dangerous activities just to feel something. It's commonly found in two types of people: drug users and serial killers.

Drug users will gradually ramp up their substance abuse levels after their tolerance to weaker drugs has built up. Similarly, a psychopath or sociopath needs to resort to seeking out the most extreme sensations possible because they're the only ones that have any effect.

He may be numb to 'everyday' sensations such as love, affection, or joyfulness, therefore, only things like murder and sexual assault make him feel anything.

When was the serial killer era?

The serial killing phenomenon in the United States was especially prominent from 1970 to 2000, which has been described as the "golden age of serial murder." The reason behind this is manyfold — encompassing everything but generally linked to the children of war. In cases like, for example, the BTK killer, his father was a returning war veteran with PTSD (Post-traumatic stress disorder). John Wayne Gacy, Jeffrey Dahmer, and Ted Bundy were all born during wartime. These children with psychopathy, sociopathy, and other serious personality disorders are basically coded for aggression and violence, low emotional empathy, low anxiety, low reactivity, etc. Those disorders can remain relatively mild if they had a good upbringing but if they were raised by abusive parents or in violent environments, all bets are off. They generally develop the personality and compulsion befitting a killer when they're young — by the time they're 14, they're basically fully formed; they generally start killing in their late twenties. However, the number of active serial killers in the country peaked in 1989 and has been steadily trending downward since.

FAMOUS
SERIAL KILLERS

Backgrounds - Motives - Victims

TED BUNDY

1946-1989

Birthplace

Burlington

Zodiac Sign

Sagittarius

Modus Operandi

Abduction

Rape

Strangulation

Confessed Victims

28-30

Ted Bundy, in full Theodore Robert Bundy, was born on November 24, 1946 in Burlington, Vermont, the U.S. and died January 24, 1989 in Starke, Florida.

Compared to the rest of his family, Bundy had the best relationship with his mother. However, Bundy expressed that he always had a feeling of being unloved upon his capture. When his mom married his stepfather, she had 4 more children, which might have caused Bundy to get a feeling of abandonment. His illegitimacy may have also led him to grow resentful towards his mother in his younger years.

Psychiatrists who took part in the case of Ted Bundy said that such actions and doings can only occur to those who were seriously traumatized when they were seriously traumatized when they were kids. They may have also been grave victims of abuse or they may have seen extreme violence from family members. With this, experts have suggested that his grandfather Simon Cowell could have molested him as a child. According to childhood friend Sandi Holt, Bundy always got teased as a boy because of his speech impediment. As a result, Bundy never really fit in as a kid. Although he was an average athlete, he never made it to any of the varsity tryouts in high school. That said, Bundy spent most of his childhood and formative years as a loner.

In college, Bundy dated Stephanie Brooks, whose real name is Diane Edwards. They fell in love for a brief while, but Brooks broke up with him due to his crazy streaks, lack of ambition, and immature ways. Later on, reports show that his victims all had the same physical appearance as that of his ex-girlfriend. Tragically, all were white females aged 15-25 years with long, brown hair.

Ted Bundy was the definition of a two-faced person. One moment he could be the nicest guy in the world who didn't have any trouble luring young women to his car to give a helping hand, only to beat them over the head a moment later to commit his despicable crimes. Despite this apparent stability, he sexually assaulted and killed several young women in Washington, Oregon, Colorado, Utah, and Florida between 1974 and 1978. Some estimated that he was responsible for hundreds of deaths. In one of his trials, Bundy admitted to photographing the corpses of his victims. More disturbingly, he decapitated 12 of his victims' heads and kept them as souvenirs as reminders of his "hard work." He was sentenced to death in 1979 for the murder of two college students. In the following year, he again was sentenced to death, this time for the rape and murder of a 12-year-old girl.

In June 1977, during a pre-trial hearing, he escaped by jumping out of the law library window. He was captured a week later. On December 30, 1977, Bundy escaped from prison and made his way to Tallahassee, Florida where he rented an apartment near Florida State University under the name Chris Hagen. Bundy asked Carole Ann Boone to marry him while she was standing as a witness and Ted defended himself as his lawyer. Surprisingly, Boone said yes. She even gave birth to their daughter just over a year after Bundy was sentenced to death.

He was executed in Florida's electric chair in 1989.

ED GEIN

1906-1984

Birthplace
Plainfield

Zodiac Sign
Virgo

Modus Operandi
Shooting
Post-mortem
mutilation

Confirmed Victims
2

Ed Gein, in full Edward Theodore Gein, also called the Butcher of Plainfield, was born on August 27, 1906, in Plainfield, Wisconsin, the U.S. and died on July 26, 1984, in Madison, Wisconsin.

Gein endured a difficult childhood. His father was an alcoholic, and his mother was verbally abusive toward him. Ed Gein's mother would often read bible verses to her son and would preach about the evil of the world. She also convinced him that all women were impure except for her.

In 1944, his brother Henry died in mysterious circumstances during a fire near the family's farm in Plainfield. Although Gein reported his brother missing to the police, he was able to lead them directly to the burned body when they arrived. Despite bruises discovered on the victim's head, the death was ruled an accident. Following his mother's death, Ed Gein transformed the house into something of a shrine to her memory. He boarded up rooms that she'd used, keeping them in pristine condition, and moved into a small bedroom off the kitchen. Living alone, far from town, he began to sink into his obsessions. Ed filled his days by learning about Nazi medical experiments, studying human anatomy, consuming porn — though he never attempted to date any real-life women — and reading horror novels. He also began to indulge his sick fantasies.

Indeed, for a full decade, no one thought much about the Gein farm outside of town. Everything changed in November 1957 when a local hardware store owner named Bernice Worden vanished, leaving nothing behind but bloodstains. The investigators found Bernice Worden in Ed's kitchen. She was dead, decapitated, and hung by her ankles from the rafters.

There were also countless bones, both whole and fragmented, skulls impaled on his bedposts, and bowls and kitchen utensils made from skulls. Worse than the bones, however, were the household items that Ed had made from human skin.

Ed Gein readily admitted that he'd collected most of the remains from three local graveyards, which he'd started to visit two years after Augusta's death. He told police he'd gone to the graveyards in a daze, looking for bodies that he thought resembled his mother. Ed told authorities that he had wanted to create a "woman suit" so that he could "become" his mother, and crawl into her skin.

He was found not guilty by reason of insanity in 1957 and sent to the Central State Hospital for the Criminally Insane, where he was diagnosed with schizophrenia. Then, his farmhouse mysteriously burned to the ground.

Until he died in 1984 at the age of 77, he only ever confessed to killing two women: tavern owner Mary Hogan in 1954 and hardware store owner Bernice Worden in 1957. The other bodies — and police found as many as 40 in his home — he claimed he'd robbed from graves.

Gein died at the Mendota Mental Health Institute due to respiratory failure secondary to lung cancer. Over the years, souvenir seekers chipped pieces from his gravestone at the Plainfield Cemetery, until the stone itself was stolen in 2000. It was recovered in June 2001, near Seattle, Washington.

EDMUND KEMPER

1948-

Birthplace
Burbank

Zodiac Sign
Sagittarius

Modus Operandi
Varied
Post-mortem decapitation

Confirmed Victims
8

Ed Kemper, in full Edmund Emil Kemper III, was born on December 18, 1948, in Burbank, California, the U.S.

After his parents' divorce in 1957, he moved with his mother and two sisters to Montana. Kemper had a difficult relationship with his alcoholic mother, as she was very critical of him, and he blamed her for all of his problems. When he was 10 years old, she forced him to live in the basement, away from his sisters, whom she feared he might harm in some way.

Signs of trouble began to emerge early. Kemper had a dark fantasy life, sometimes dreaming about killing his mother. He cut off the heads of his sisters' dolls and even coerced the girls into playing a game he called "gas chamber," in which he had them blindfold him and lead him to a chair, where he pretended to writhe in agony until he "died." His mother sent the troubled teenager Edmund to live with his paternal grandparents in North Fork, California. He hated living on his grandparents' farm. Before going to North Fork, he had already begun learning about firearms, but his grandparents took away his rifle after he killed several birds and other small animals.

At the age of 15, he shot his grandmother in the kitchen after an argument, and when his grandfather returned home, Kemper went outside and shot him in his car and then hid the body. For his crimes, Kemper was handed over to the California Youth Authority. He underwent a variety of tests, which determined that he had a very high IQ, but also suffered from paranoid schizophrenia. Kemper was eventually sent to Atascadero State Hospital, a maximum-security facility for mentally ill convicts.

In 1969, Kemper was released at the age of 21. Despite his prison doctors' recommendation that he not live with his mother, because of her past abuse and his psychological issues involving her, he rejoined her in Santa Cruz, California, where she had moved after ending her third marriage to take a job with the University of California. While there, Kemper attended community college for a time and worked a variety of jobs, eventually finding employment with the Department of Transportation in 1971. Kemper had applied to become a state trooper, but he was rejected because of his size — he weighed around 300 pounds and was 6 feet 9 inches tall, which led to his nickname "Big Ed." However, he did hang around some of the Santa Cruz police officers.

The same year he began working for the highway department, Kemper was hit by a car while out on his motorcycle. His arm was badly injured, and he received a $15,000 settlement in the civil suit he filed against the car's driver.

Unable to work, Kemper turned his mind toward other pursuits. At first, Kemper picked up female hitchhikers and let them go. However, when he offered a ride to two Fresno State students — Mary Ann Pesce and Anita Luchessa — they would never make it to their destination. Their families reported them missing soon thereafter, but nothing would be known of their fates until August 15, when a female head was discovered in the woods near Santa Cruz and was later identified as Pesce's. Luchessa's remains, however, were never found. Kemper would later explain that he stabbed and strangled Pesce before stabbing Luchessa as well. After the murders, he brought the bodies back to his apartment and removed their heads and hands. Kemper also reportedly engaged in sexual activity with their corpses.

Later that year, in September 1972, Kemper picked up 15-year-old Aiko Koo, who had decided to hitchhike rather than wait for the bus to take her to a dance class. She would meet the same fate as Pesce and Luchessa. In January 1973, Kemper continued to act on his murderous impulses, picking up hitchhiker Cindy Schall, whom he shot and killed. While his mother was out, Kemper went to her home and hid Schall's body in his room. He dismembered her corpse there the following day and threw the parts into the ocean. Several parts were later discovered when they washed up onshore. He buried her head in his mother's backyard.

In February 1973, Kemper used a campus parking sticker his mother had given him to facilitate a double-murder. He drove to the university, where he offered a ride to two students, Rosalind Thorpe and Alice Liu. Shortly after picking them up, he shot the two young women and then drove past the campus security at the gates with the two mortally wounded women in his car. After the murders, Kemper decapitated his two victims and further dismembered the bodies, removed the bullets from their heads, and disposed of their parts in different locations. In March, some of Thorpe's and Liu's remains were discovered by hikers near Highway 1 in San Mateo County.

On Good Friday 1973, he went to his mother's home, where the two had an unpleasant exchange. Kemper attacked his mother after she went to sleep, first striking her in the head with a hammer, and then cutting her throat with a knife. As he had with his other victims, he then decapitated her and cut off her hands, but then also removed her larynx and put it down the garbage disposal. After hiding his mother's body parts, Kemper called his mother's friend Sally Hallett and invited her over to the house. Kemper strangled Hallett shortly after she arrived and hid her body in a closet.

Kemper fled the area the next day, driving east until he reached Pueblo, Colorado, where on April 23 he made a call to the Santa Cruz police to confess his crimes. At first, they did not believe that the guy they knew as "Big Ed" was a killer. But during subsequent interrogations, he would lead them to all the evidence they needed to prove that he was the infamous "Co-ed Killer."

Charged with eight counts of first-degree murder, Kemper went on trial for his crimes in October 1973. He was found guilty of all of the charges in early November. When asked by the judge what he thought his punishment should be, Kemper said that he should be tortured to death. He instead received eight concurrent life sentences.

Kemper remains among the general population in prison and is considered a model prisoner. He was in charge of scheduling other inmates' appointments with psychiatrists and was an accomplished craftsman of ceramic cups. He was also a prolific reader of audiobooks for the blind. A famous article once stated that he was the coordinator of the prison's program and had personally spent over 5,000 hours narrating books with several hundred completed recordings to his name. However, he retired from the role in 2015 after suffering a stroke.

At present, Kemper is serving his time at California Medical Facility in Vacaville.

1960-2013

Birthplace

El Paso

Zodiac Sign

Pisces

Modus Operandi

Home intrusion

Raping

Shooting

Confirmed Victims

13

Richard Ramirez, in full Ricardo Leyva Munoz Ramirez, also known as Night Stalker, was born on February 29, 1960, in El Paso, in Texas, the U.S. and died on June 7, 2013, in Greenbrae, California.

Richard Ramirez was the youngest of five children born to Mexican immigrants. His dad treated him so poorly that he would tie him to a cross in a graveyard overnight as a form of punishment.

According to reports, when he was about 12 years old, a cousin who was a Vietnam War veteran showed him pictures of Vietnamese women he had allegedly raped, tortured, and killed. The following year, Ramirez was a witness to his cousin's fatal shooting of his wife. Around this time, Ramirez began breaking into home.

After dropping out of high school, he moved to Los Angeles. He continued to commit crimes and was briefly imprisoned for stealing a car. In June 1984, Ramirez committed his first known murder, raping and stabbing a 79-year-old widow. He had a pattern — he killed the man in the house, and sexually assaulted a woman, and always made sure he could see the fear in his victim's eyes. He then apparently waited some eight months before resuming his killings. Most of the deaths occurred in the Los Angeles area and took place during home invasions.

He used a wide variety of weapons and different murder methods, including handguns, various types of knives, a machete, a tire iron, and a claw hammer. He was known to attack by punching, pistol-whipping, and strangling many of his victims, both manually with his hands and in one instance a ligature; stomped at least one victim to death in her sleep, and tortured another victim by shocking her with a live electrical cord.

Ramirez also enjoyed frequently degrading and humiliating his victims, especially those who survived his attacks or whom he explicitly decided not to kill, by forcing them to profess that they loved Satan, or telling them to "swear on Satan" if there were no more valuables left in their homes he had broken into and burglarized. Ramirez do not spare children. Earlier on in his killing spree, there were a series of young children being taken from their beds, assaulted, and then abandoned.

The "Night Stalker," as the killer became known, created a panic that saw a surge in gun sales. Eventually, a fingerprint was discovered that led to Ramirez's identification. On August 30, 1985—six days after his last known murder—Ramirez's name and photograph were released to the public, and the following day a man in East Los Angeles saw him and notified the police. A chase ensued, and as Ramirez tried to steal a car, he was surrounded by a crowd and beaten until police arrived. By the time of the trial, Ramirez had fans who were writing him letters and paying him visits. One of them was Doreen Lioy who wrote him nearly 75 letters during his incarceration.

On September 20, 1989, he was convicted of all charges: 13 counts of murder, 5 attempted murders, 11 sexual assaults, and 14 burglaries, although he's assumed to have committed many more crimes. He was sentenced to death — but in 2013, he died of cancer in prison, after serving 23 years on death row.

GARY RIDGWAY

1949-

Birthplace

Salt Lake City

Zodiac Sign

Aquarius

Modus Operandi

Strangulation

Necrophilia

Dumping corspes

Confessed Victims

71+

Gary Ridgway, in full Gary Leon Ridgway, also known as Green River Killer, was born on February 18, 1949, in Salt Lake City, Utah, the U.S.

Ridgway claimed that his mother engaged in inappropriate behavior when he was young. Notably, he alleged that after wetting the bed—a habit that persisted into his early teens—she would wash his genitals. At some point, he began fantasizing about killing her, and in the mid-1960s, he stabbed a young boy.

After graduating from high school in 1969—at the age of 20—Ridgway served a two-year stint in the U.S. Navy and later settled in the Seattle area, where he worked as a truck painter. Over the next 30 years, he married three times and had a son.

In 1980, Ridgway was arrested for allegedly choking a prostitute, but no charges were filed after he claimed that the woman had bit him. Two years later he was arrested for solicitation.

Ridgway was believed to have begun his killing spree shortly thereafter. His victims were prostitutes, vagrants, or women he thought they were so. All of them were aged in their mid-teens to late thirties. He would pick them up, take them somewhere secluded, have sex with them, often from behind in order to get the drop on them, and then kill them by strangling them, usually with his arm, though he later started using various ligatures such as rope, fishing line, belts, extension cords, socks, or even T-shirts when he realized that the victims could potentially leave conspicuous defensive injuries on him. Some were killed in his home or in his truck. The bodies were then dumped in the wilderness, usually nude and sometimes posed.

He had a habit of dumping them in "clusters" in different locations over a period of time, usually near some nearby landmark or in the water. He would return to the bodies to watch them decompose and change color and to engage in sexual acts with them. As a forensic countermeasure, he would scatter random trash around the crime scenes and carry some victims across the state line into Oregon to confuse the investigators.

By August 1982, police believed that a serial killer was at work, and they eventually formed a special task force. Ridgway soon became a suspect. In 1983, he was questioned about the disappearance of a prostitute who a witness claimed had gotten into his truck. Ridgway denied the allegations and passed a polygraph in 1984. In 1987, the police searched his house and took samples of his hair and saliva. Because there wasn't enough evidence to make an arrest, he was released. Ridgway's involvement in the investigation led his coworkers to nickname him "Green River Gary". As the years went by, more remains of his victims were found; the most recent finding was on December 21, 2010. In 1991, the Green River Task Force was reduced to a single person, Tom Jensen. For a decade afterwards, the case remained completely dormant. During that time, Ridgway is only confirmed to have committed a single murder.

It wasn't until 2001 that the big break in the case finally came when the murders were re-investigated with a task force consisting of 30 people, including forensic and DNA experts. A DNA comparison of semen found on the victims' bodies and the samples taken from Ridgway in 1987 was made using more recent technology and came back a match. Ridgway was consequently arrested, and charged with the murders of Opal Mills, Marcia Chapman, Carol Christensen, and Cynthia Hinds; the first three were connected to him by DNA evidence and the fourth by circumstantial evidence. Three more charges, those of Wendy Coffield, Debra Bonner, and Debra Estes, were added when the investigators found traces of a kind of spray paint Ridgway used at work on their remains.

In 2003, Ridgway made a plea bargain with the prosecution, agreeing to make a full confession and help the authorities find the remains of his victims in exchange for avoiding the death penalty. In total, he was convicted of 49 murders. He confessed to a total of 71, though some estimate that he may have killed more than 90 women. At one point during the legal proceedings when the victims' families gave testimonies, Ridgway broke into tears and told them he was sorry. Ridgway is currently serving his sentence at the Washington State Penitentiary in Walla Walla, Washington.

HAROLD SHIPMAN

1946-2004

Birthplace
Nottingham
Zodiac Sign
Capricorn
Modus Operandi
Diamorphine use
and injecting
Confirmed Victims
15

Harold Shipman, in full Harold Frederick Shipman, was born on January 14, 1946, in Nottingham, England, and died on January 13, 2004, in Wakefield, England.

He was born into a working-class family in Manchester. A bright child, he became interested in medicine as he watched his mother receive morphine injections to ease the pain she suffered while dying of lung cancer.

In 1970, he received a medical degree from Leeds University, and a few years later, he became a general practitioner in Todmorden in Lancashire. In 1975, after it was discovered that he had written several fraudulent prescriptions for the opiate pethidine, to which he had become addicted, he was forced out of his practice and into drug rehabilitation.

In 1977, Shipman found work as a general practitioner in the town of Hyde in Greater Manchester, where eventually he gained respectability and developed a thriving practice.

In 1998, one of his patients, an 81-year-old woman Deborah Massey, was discovered dead in her home only hours after Shipman visited her. Massey's family was perplexed by the suddenness of her death because she appeared to be in good health. Her will had been changed to benefit Shipman (it bequeathed her entire estate, valued at some £400,000, to him), and by his insistence that no autopsy was necessary.

In 2000, he was convicted on 15 counts of murder and one count of forgery and sentenced to life in prison. A government inquiry was ordered to determine how many more patients Shipman may have murdered; in 2005, an official report found that he had killed an estimated 250 people beginning in 1971. In most cases, Shipman injected the victim with a lethal dose of the painkiller diamorphine and then signed a death certificate attributing the incident to natural causes. His motives were unclear. Some speculated that Shipman might have been seeking to avenge the death of his mother while others suggested that he thought he was practicing euthanasia, removing from the population older people who might otherwise have become a burden to the health care system. A third possibility raised was that he derived pleasure from the knowledge that, as a doctor, he had the power of life or death over his patients and that killing was the means through which he expressed this power. Despite his forgery of the will of one of his victims, financial gain appears not to have been a serious motive.

One key question that plagued investigators was how a large number of deaths could have occurred without raising suspicions of foul play. This was all the more baffling because Shipman's patients were normally healthy shortly before their encounters with him. The fact that Shipman took advantage of his patients' trust in him as a doctor made his crimes particularly odious to the public.

In the end, Harold was believed to have killed himself in his cell on the eve of his 58th birthday in 2004, planned his death so his wife Primrose - who continued to visit him every week after his conviction in 2000 - could receive the maximum pension payout £100,000.

JEFFREY DAHMER

1960-1994

Birthplace

Milwaukee

Zodiac Sign

Gemini

Modus Operandi

Rape

Strangulation

Cannibalism

Confessed Victims

17

Jeffrey Dahmer, in full Jeffrey Lionel Dahmer, was born on May 21, 1960, in Milwaukee, Wisconsin, the U.S. and died on November 28, 1994, in Portage, Wisconsin.

He was a happy child who enjoyed typical toddler activities. However, after he underwent hernia surgery at a very young age, his personality began to change from a jubilant social child to a loner who was uncommunicative and withdrawn. His facial expressions transformed from sweet smiles to a emotionless stare—a look that remained with him throughout his life.

In 1966, the Dahmers moved to Bath, Ohio. His insecurities grew after the move and his shyness kept him from making many friends. While his peers were busy listening to the latest songs,

Dahmer was busy collecting roadkill and stripping the animal carcasses, and saving the bones. Dahmer continued being a loner during his years at Revere High School. He had average grades, worked in the school newspaper, and developed a dangerous drinking problem. His parents, struggling with issues of their own, divorced when Jeffrey was almost 18. He remained living with his father, who traveled often and was busy nurturing a relationship with his new wife.

On June 6, 1978, Dahmer committed his first murder. While living alone in the family home, Dahmer invited an 18-year-old hitchhiker named Steven Hicks for drinks. After several hours of drinking, Hicks wanted to leave and Dahmer did not want him to. When he tried to leave, Dahmer bludgeoned and strangled him to death with a barbell. He then dismembered his body with a carving knife, removed the flesh off his bones, and smashed them with a sledgehammer, spreading the pieces all over his backyard afterward. His second victim Steven Tuomi was beaten to death while the former was in a drunken state.

Dahmer would visit gay bars, gay libraries, and the local mall, or walk the streets, looking for victims and invite them to his apartment to have sex or drink while watching pornography.

All of the victims were aged in their mid-teens to mid-thirties, a majority of them being bi- or homosexual, of African or Asian descent and lived "high-risk" lifestyles. A lot of them also had criminal records, often for serious crimes such as arson, rape, battery, and sexual assault.

After picking them up, he would bring them home, and drug them by crushing prescription drugs and blending it with their drinks. Afterward, he would usually rape them, murder them by strangling them with his bare hands or with a leather strap, and dismember the remains in his bathtub. He would then remove the organs from his victim's chest, suspend the torsos to allow the blood to drain in the bathtub, and remove the flesh from the body with a knife. He would also engage in sexual acts with the bodies, pose and take pictures of them, and eventually dispose of their flesh by dissolving them in chemicals to the point that they were completely liquefied and could be poured down a toilet or a sink. He would also keep several body parts in his apartment, usually the heads and genitals, even preserving whole bodies in large, chemical-filled vats.

He eventually attempted to turn some of them into "zombies" by drilling holes in their skulls and injecting hydrochloric acid or boiling hot water into their temporal lobes using large syringes, which would prove to be fatal for Konerak Sinthasomphone and Jeremiah Weinberger. The heads, with which he had a particular fascination, were often boiled until the flesh came off, preserved with Soilex (a laundry detergent) mixed with water and bleach solutions, and painted to make them look like they were made of plastic. He would also consume many of his victims, eating parts of them such as their hearts, livers, and biceps. During the entire process, he would drink alcohol. His murders were motivated by powerful abandonment issues rooted in his fear of rejection and loss and a need for control. The cannibalism he practiced, consuming his victims to make them a part of himself, was an extension of his need for power.

Dahmer was caught when the 32-year-old Tracy Edwards escaped from his apartment and alerted police that Dahmer was trying to kill him.

Finally, Dahmer confessed to 17 murders in all, dating back to his first victim in 1978. On November 28, 1994, he was beaten to death by Christopher Scarver, a fellow inmate at the Columbia Correctional Institution in Portage, Wisconsin.

JOHN WAYNE GACY

1942-1994

Birthplace

Chicago

Zodiac Sign

Pisces

Modus Operandi

Rape and torture

Stabbing

Asphyxiation

Confirmed Victims

33+

John Wayne Gacy was born on March 17, 1942, in Chicago, Illinois, the U.S. and died on May 10, 1994, in Statesville, Illinois.

His first memory as a child was his father beating him with a belt. The second was his father striking him across the head with a broomstick to the point he was knocked unconscious. Because of the serious neglect and abuse he suffered from his father, the little Wayne was drawn to his mother, Marion, and his two sisters. This did not do him any good though because this allowed his father to insult him as being a "Mama's boy" and "sissy".

As a teenager, John Wayne Gacy was overweight and suffered from a heart condition. In the 4 years of high school, he spent almost 3 years in hospital beds.

Gacy briefly moved to Las Vegas where he found a job that would awaken something sinister within him, a janitor in a mortuary. While working at the Palm Mortuary in Las Vegas, he later confessed that he actually committed two acts of necrophilia with two young deceased males.

Despite his homosexual encounters with the deceased bodies of two young men, Gacy went back home in the early 1960s and acquired a degree in a business school. He found a job as a salesman and was so good at his job that he was promoted to the local manager of a company. He married twice and had two children.

According to Gacy's confession to the police, he would pick up male runaways or male prostitutes in their mid-teens to their early twenties from the Chicago Greyhound Bus station or off the streets. Afterward, he would take them back to his house by either promising them money for sex, offering them a job with his construction company, simply grabbing them by force or forcing them into his car at gunpoint.

Once they got back to his house, he would handcuff them or tie them up in another way after intoxicating them with alcohol or knocking them out with chloroform. He would torture them in various ways (such as using a fire poker on them, dripping hot melted candle wax on their bodies, repeatedly drowning them in his bathtub, or placing them in a homemade "rack"). As a show of dominance, he would urinate on his victims. Gacy would rape his victims both before and after killing them, keeping the bodies around for a day or so.

One of his most infamous ways of binding his victims was convincing them to allow him to handcuff them under the pretense that it was part of a magic trick. Gacy would often stick paper towels or clothing in their mouths to muffle their screams, causing them to fatally asphyxiate. He would also kill his victims by strangling them with a rope or a board as he sexually assaulted them with sex toys, then bury the bodies in his crawlspace.

It took a missing beloved honors student to really break the investigation open. When Robert Piest vanished in December 1978, the public concern was high and police were positive, he was no runaway. He was convicted of 33 murders (by one individual). On death row at Menard Correctional Center, he spent much of his time painting. He was executed by lethal injection at Stateville Correctional Center on May 10, 1994.

AILEEN WUORNOS

1956-2002

Birthplace

Rochester

Zodiac Sign

Pisces

Modus Operandi

Shooting

Robbing

Confirmed Victims

7

Aileen Wuornos, in full Aileen Carol Wuornos, originally Aileen Pittman, was born on February 29, 1956, in Rochester, Michigan, the U.S. and died on October 9, 2002, in Starke, Florida.

Wuornos had a deeply troubled childhood. Her parents separated before her birth, and her father later spent time in mental hospitals for child molestation. When Wuornos was 4 years old, she and her brother were sent to live with her grandparents. She has claimed that she was sexually abused by her grandfather who also allegedly beat her.

At school, she was also engaging in sex with boys in exchange for loose change and cigarettes. The money she earned from selling her body at a young age was used to buy alcohol and food.

In 1970, when she was only 14, Wuornos was allegedly raped by a friend of her grandfather's and became pregnant. She gave birth the following year and put the baby up for adoption. Following the death of her grandmother, Wuornos was thrown out of the house and forced to make it on her own. She was only 15-years-old and dropped out of school to support herself the only way she knew how—prostitution.

In 1974, Wuornos was imprisoned for driving while intoxicated and for firing a gun from a moving vehicle. She subsequently was arrested numerous times on charges that included armed robbery, check forgery, and auto theft.

One bright spot in Wuornos's dark history is her brief union with wealthy yacht club owner Lewis Fell, 69. When the two married in Florida in 1976, their nuptials were even printed in the society pages. However, shortly after he annulled the marriage and filed a restraining order against Wuornos when she attacked him with his cane.

Wuornos' first known victim was 51-year-old Richard Mallory. In 1989, Wuornos was picked up by Mallory and according to her testimony, she was tied to the steering wheel and repeatedly attacked. She managed to retrieve her gun from her purse and shot him three times with a .22 pistol in self-defense. She then dumped his body in the woodlands and stole his Cadillac. Wuornos targeted males between the ages of 40-65. She would lure them with promises of sex and kill them by shooting. She sometimes undressed them post-mortem and take personal possessions from them to later sell.

Arrested in early 1991, she admitted to the killings but claimed that she acted in self-defense after the men assaulted her. Supporters of Wuornos viewed her as a strong independent woman—and even as a heroic figure for defending herself against male aggression. In 1992, she was convicted of one of the murders and sentenced to death. During the death penalty phase of the trial, expert psychologist Dr. Bernard testified that Wuornos suffered from borderline personality disorder and antisocial personality disorder. At the time of the crimes, she had impaired capacity and mental disturbance; linked to a history of sexual abuse throughout her childhood and adolescence.

On October 9th, 2002, Wuornos was executed at the Florida State Prison at 9:47 am. She declined a last meal and instead had a cup of coffee.

DENNIS RADER

1945–

Birthplace
Pittsburg
Zodiac Sign
Pisces
Modus Operandi
Home invasion
Asphyxiation
Stabbing
Confirmed Victims
10

Dennis Rader, in full Dennis Lynn Rader, also known as BTK Killer, was born on March 9, 1945, in Pittsburg, Kansas, the U.S. He called himself BTK because he bound, tortured, and killed his victims.

Rader admits to having killed cats and dogs by hanging and strangling them as a youth. During puberty, he already dreamed of tying girls up and having sex with them. He says that his fantasies were "almost like a picture show" that he wanted to direct and produce, no matter what the cost.

The only social activities that Rader indulged in during his youth were related to his Lutheran church or the boy scouts. While he was a boy scout, he learned the art of tying knots that would help him later in life when he bound his victims before killing them. In the 1960s. he served in the U.S. Air Force, and in 1970 he returned to Wichita, where he married and had two children. He held various jobs, including a brief stint as a factory worker for the Coleman Company, a maker of camping equipment. In 1979, he graduated from Wichita State University, where he studied criminal justice. During this time he began working for ADT, a home-security company, and in 1991 he became a compliance officer in Park City, Kansas. Rader was active in his church, and he served as a Boy Scout leader.

In January 1974, he committed his first murders, strangling four family members, including two children, in their Wichita home; the mother had worked for Coleman. Semen was found at the scene, though none of the victims had been sexually assaulted. He took a watch from the home, and he would acquire souvenirs—often underwear—from subsequent victims.

In April 1974, Rader targeted a 21-year-old woman who was another Coleman employee. After breaking into her house; however, he also encountered her brother, who managed to escape despite being shot. Rader fatally stabbed the woman before fleeing. Later that year, he wrote a letter detailing the

January murders and saying that "the code words for me will be...bind them, torture them, kill them, B.T.K." He left the note in a book at the Wichita Public Library, and it was eventually recovered by the police.

Over the next two decades, Rader killed five more women. His sixth victim was strangled in March 1977 after he locked her three young children in the bathroom. Following the death of his next victim in December 1977, Rader grew irritated by the lack of media coverage.

Rader then waited eight years before murdering a neighbor in her home in 1985; he reportedly later took her body to his church, where he photographed her in bondage. A 28-year-old mother of two was killed in 1986, and in 1991, Rader committed his last murder, strangling a 62-year-old woman in her secluded home. The cases subsequently went cold.

In 2004, on the 30th anniversary of Rader's first murders, a local paper ran a feature in which it speculated that the killer had either died or been imprisoned. Rader responded by sending various evidence from his ninth murder—notably a copy of the victim's driver's license as well as photographs of her body—to a reporter. For the next year, he sent packages to the media or simply left items around Wichita. He often used cereal boxes—possibly a reference to "serial killer"—to hold drawings; crime souvenirs, including photographs; written descriptions of the murders; and even dolls, posed to mimic the various deaths.

In January 2005, police received a break after recovering a cereal box that included a note in which Rader asked police whether they would be able to trace a floppy disk he wanted to send them. Through a classified ad, law enforcement officials indicated that it would be safe. He then sent them a disk, which the police quickly traced to his church, where he served as president of the congregation.

Rader's DNA was then matched to the semen found at the first crime scene. He was arrested in February 2005, and he soon confessed to the crimes—and expressed shock that the police had lied to him.

He was arrested in February 2005, and he soon confessed to the crimes—and expressed shock that the police had lied to him. He was sentenced to 10 consecutive life sentences, with a minimum of 175 years in 2005.

DAVID BERKOWITZ

1953-

Birthplace

Brooklyn

Zodiac Sign

Gemini

Modus Operandi

Arson (past)

Shooting

Confirmed Victims

6

David Berkowitz, in full David Richard Berkowitz, also known as Son of Sam, original name David Falco, was born June 1, 1953, in Brooklyn, New York, the U.S.

Berkowitz's birth parents were Joseph Kleinman and Betty Broder. At the time of his birth, Broder had recently been abandoned by her husband, Tony Falco, for another woman. She started an affair with Kleinman, a married real estate agent. Because of this, Broder listed Falco as the father on Berkowitz's birth certificate. Berkowitz was later adopted by Nathan and Pearl Berkowitz.

His erratic behavior, which began after the death of his adoptive mother in 1967, intensified when his adoptive father remarried in 1971 and moved to Florida without him.

In 1971, Berkowitz joined the army, and he became an excellent marksman before he left the service in 1974.

Even though the murder spree officially started in July 1976, he already committed a heinous crime the year before. On Christmas Eve of the year 1975, he stabbed two girls in Co-op City. The youngest victim, a 15-year-old girl named Michelle Forman, was stabbed severely and had to stay in the hospital for 7 days before recovering from her wounds. He actively sought out young females to murder and committed his crimes in the New York boroughs of the Bronx, Queens, and Brooklyn. His weapon of choice was a .44 caliber Bulldog revolver - in fact, one of his nicknames was the .44 Caliber Killer.

He was arrested on August 10, 1977, and subsequently indicted for eight shootings. He confessed to all of them, and initially claimed to have been obeying the orders of a demon manifested in the form of a dog belonging to his neighbor "Sam". Also. when the police searched his apartment in Yonkers, New York, they found a diary that featured detailed descriptions of hundreds of arsons that he committed all over New York City. On May 8, 1978, he pleaded guilty; in June he was sentenced to 365 years in prison.

JACK THE RIPPER

Unknown

Birthplace
Presumably London

Gender
Presumably male

Modus Operandi
Throat slashing

Confirmed Victims
5

Jack the Ripper, a pseudonymous murderer of at least five women in or near the Whitechapel district of London's East End between August and November 1888. The case is one of the most famous mysteries of English crime.

Some dozen murders between 1888 and 1892 have been speculatively attributed to Jack the Ripper, but only five of those, all committed in 1888, were linked by police to a single murderer.

The body of Mary Ann Nichols was discovered at about 3:40 a.m. on Friday 31 August 1888 in Buck's Row (now Durward Street), Whitechapel. Nichols had last been seen alive approximately one hour before the discovery of her body by a Mrs. Emily, with whom she had previously shared a bed at a common lodging-house in in Thrawl Street, Spitalfields, walking in the direction of Whitechapel Road. Her throat was severed by two deep cuts, one of which completely severed all the tissue down to the vertebrae. Her vagina had been stabbed twice, and the lower part of her abdomen was partly ripped open by a deep, jagged wound, causing her bowels to protrude. Several other incisions inflicted to both sides of her abdomen had also been caused by the same knife; each of these wounds had been inflicted in a downward thrusting manner.

One week later, on Saturday 8 September 1888, the body of Annie Chapman was discovered at approximately 6 a.m. near the steps to the doorway of the backyard of 29 Hanbury Street, Spitalfields. As in the case of Mary Ann Nichols, the throat was severed by two deep cuts. Her abdomen had been cut entirely open, with a section of the flesh from her stomach being placed upon her left shoulder and another section of skin and flesh—plus her small intestines—being removed and placed above her right shoulder. Chapman's autopsy also revealed that her uterus and sections of her bladder and vagina had been removed.

At the inquest into Chapman's murder, Elizabeth Long

described having seen Chapman standing outside 29 Hanbury Street at about 5:30 a.m. in the company of a dark-haired man wearing a brown deerstalker hat and dark overcoat, and of a "shabby-genteel" appearance. According to this eyewitness, the man had asked Chapman the question, "Will you?" to which Chapman had replied, "Yes."

Elizabeth Stride and Catherine Eddowes were both killed in the early morning hours of Sunday 30 September 1888. Stride's body was discovered at approximately 1 a.m. in Dutfield's Yard, off Berner Street (now Henriques Street) in Whitechapel. The cause of death was a single clear-cut incision, measuring six inches across her neck which had severed her left carotid artery and her trachea before terminating beneath her right jaw.

The absence of any further mutilations to her body has led to uncertainty as to whether Stride's murder was committed by the Ripper, or whether he was interrupted during the attack. Several witnesses later informed police they had seen Stride in the company of a man in or close to Berner Street on the evening of 29 September and in the early hours of 30 September, but each gave differing descriptions: some said that her companion was fair, others dark; some said that he was shabbily dressed, others well-dressed. Eddowes's body was found in a corner of Mitre Square in the City of London, three-quarters of an hour after the discovery of the body of Elizabeth Stride. Her throat was severed from ear to ear and her abdomen ripped open by a long, deep, and jagged wound before her intestines had been placed over her right shoulder, with a section of the intestine being completely detached and placed between her body and left arm.

The left kidney and the major part of Eddowes's uterus had been removed, and her face had been disfigured, with her nose severed, her cheek slashed, and cuts measuring a quarter of an inch and a half an inch respectively vertically incised through each of her eyelids. A triangular incision—the apex of which pointed towards Eddowes's eye—had also been carved upon each of her cheeks, and a section of the auricle and lobe of her right ear was later recovered from her clothing. The police surgeon who conducted the post-mortem upon Eddowes's body stated his opinion these mutilations would have taken "at least five minutes' ' to complete.

A local cigarette salesman named Joseph Lawende had passed through the square with two friends shortly before the murder, and he described seeing a fair-haired man of shabby appearance with a woman who may have been Eddowes. Lawende's companions were unable to confirm his description. The murders of Stride and Eddowes ultimately became known as the "double event".

A section of Eddowes's bloodied apron was found at the entrance to a tenement in Goulston Street, Whitechapel, at 2:55 a.m. A chalk inscription upon the wall directly above this piece of apron read: "The Juwes are The men That Will not be Blamed for nothing." This graffito became known as the Goulston Street graffito. The message appeared to imply that a Jew or Jews, in general, were responsible for the series of murders, but it is unclear whether the graffito was written by the murderer on dropping the section of an apron, or was merely incidental and had nothing to do with the case. Such graffiti were commonplace in Whitechapel. Police Commissioner Charles Warren feared that the graffito might spark anti-semitic riots and ordered the writing washed away before dawn.

The extensively mutilated and disemboweled body of Mary Jane Kelly was discovered lying on the bed in the single room where she lived at 13 Miller's Court, off Dorset Street,

Spitalfields, at 10:45 a.m. on Friday 9 November 1888. Her face had been "hacked beyond all recognition", with her throat severed down to the spine, and the abdomen almost emptied of its organs. Her uterus, kidneys and one breast had been placed beneath her head, and other viscera from her body placed beside her foot, about the bed, and sections of her abdomen and thighs upon a bedside table. The heart was missing from the crime scene. Multiple ashes found within the fireplace at 13 Miller's Court suggested Kelly's murderer had burned several combustible items to illuminate the single room as he mutilated her body. A recent fire had been severe enough to melt the solder between a kettle and its spout, which had fallen into the grate of the fireplace.

The name "Jack the Ripper" originated in a letter written by an individual claiming to be the murderer that was disseminated in the media. The letter is widely believed to have been a hoax and may have been written by journalists in an attempt to heighten interest in the story. The public came increasingly to believe in a single serial killer known as "Jack the Ripper", mainly because of both the extraordinarily brutal nature of the murders and media coverage of the crimes.

☠
ZODIAC KILLER

‖ Unknown ‖

Birthplace
Presumably America

Gender
Presumably male

Modus Operandi
Shooting

Stabbing

Suspected Victims
5-37 killed

Zodiac Killer is an unidentified American serial killer who is believed to have murdered at least five people in northern California between 1968 and 1969.

From the accounts of the few survivors of known Zodiac attacks, it is generally believed that the Zodiac dressed in black clothing of various types (depending on the month), and, at least on one occasion, wore a dark hood decorated with the Zodiac symbol.

His methods varied also, with some victims being dispatched by an automatic pistol (of several types) or bladed weapons, most notably what was probably a military-style knife. According to one of his letters, he, during the Christmas killings, had a pencil-sized flashlight taped to his gun to be able to shoot in the dark. David Faraday, age 17, was shot once in the head at point-blank range and died within minutes. Betty Lou Jensen, age 16, was shot five times in the back and killed instantly. The weapon was a .22 caliber semi-automatic pistol. The ammunition was Winchester Western Super X copper-coated long rifle. Darlene Ferrin, age 22, was shot five times. Mike Mageau, age 19, was shot four times. The weapon was a 9mm semi-automatic pistol. Cecelia Shepard, age 22, was stabbed 10 times, five in the front and five in the back. Bryan Hartnell, age 20, was stabbed six times in the back. The knife had a wooden handle and a blade, approximately 10 to 12 inches long.

Cab driver Paul Stine, age 29, was shot once in the head at point-blank range. The weapon was a 9mm semi-automatic pistol, not the same 9mm used in the Ferrin murder. There were three witnesses from a house on the southeast corner of the intersection. Ray Davis, age 27, was shot twice from behind in his own cab. The weapon was of .22 caliber and the ammunition came from a long rifle.

A 1966 graduate of Riverside's Ramona High School, 18-year-old Cheri Jo Bates was beaten and stabbed multiple times with a short-bladed knife. Her throat was also cut. There was no evidence of robbery or sexual molestation. There were no witnesses.

The Zodac Killer, most likely intentionally, acted in locations where jurisdictions overlapped, as a mean of slowing down the authorities. In one of his letters, he claimed to have killed some of his victims "by fire" and "by rope". Though cases involving strangulation were linked to the Zodiac (the Santa Rosa hitchhiker murders), no cases involving arson were ever linked to him. His letters, sent from 1969 to 1974, were signed with a symbol resembling the crosshairs of a gunsight and typically began with the phrase, "this is the Zodiac speaking." Included among the letters were four ciphers or cryptograms, the first of which was sent in three parts to three Bay Area newspapers in July 1969.

Known as the "408 cipher" for the number of characters it contained, it was soon decoded by a pair of private citizens. Its message stated in part, "I like killing people because it is so much fun." Another cipher, the "340 cipher," mailed to the San Francisco Chronicle in November 1969, was finally decoded in 2020 by a team of three amateur code breakers; the message was revealed:

"I HOPE YOU ARE HAVING LOTS OF FUN IN TRYING TO CATCH ME

THAT WASNT ME ON THE TV SHOW

WHICH BRINGS UP A POINT ABOUT ME

I AM NOT AFRAID OF THE GAS CHAMBER

BECAUSE IT WILL SEND ME TO PARADICE ALL THE SOONER

BECAUSE I NOW HAVE ENOUGH SLAVES TO WORK FOR ME

WHERE EVERYONE ELSE HAS NOTHING WHEN THEY REACH PARADICE

SO THEY ARE AFRAID OF DEATH

I AM NOT AFRAID BECAUSE I KNOW THAT MY NEW LIFE IS

LIFE WILL BE AN EASY ONE IN PARADICE DEATH"

In one of his last taunting letters to the news media, the Zodiac Killer claimed he had 37 victims to show for his five years of terrorizing the San Francisco Bay Area.

One nerve-wracking fact about the Zodiac Killer is that his prints or DNA were never found on any of his crime scenes. In one of his letters, he explained that he used airplane model cement on his fingers to disguise his fingerprint.

RODNEY ALCALA

1943-2021

Birthplace
San Antonio

Zodiac Sign
Virgo

Modus Operandi
Raping
Strangulation

Confirmed Victims
5

Rodney Alcala, in full Rodney James Alcala, was born as Rodrigo Jacques Alcala-Buquor in San Antonio, Texas, on August 23, 1943 and died on July 24, 2021.

He moved to Mexico with his family when he was around eight and his father abandoned the family while they were in Mexico. Alcala, his siblings, and his mother later relocated to Los Angeles.

At the age of 17, Rodney joined the 'US Army' and worked as a clerk. In 1964, he was diagnosed with an antisocial personality disorder after a nervous breakdown. He was later diagnosed with various disorders, such as narcissistic personality and borderline personality disorder. He also showed traits of sexual sadism comorbidities and psychopathy. However, despite this, he attended the 'UCLA School of Fine Arts' and later studied film at New York University (NYU), where he was mentored by director Roman Polanski.

After fleeing the scene of his 1968 attack on 8-year-old Tali Shapiro, Alcala traveled to the East Coast. In 1971 he was included on the FBI's Most Wanted list. Some girls at an arts camp in New Hampshire recognized their counselor, who was using the name, John Berger, from this list. They told the camp's dean and Alcala was soon arrested. He served just 34 months for the charge of child molestation. Though he was a registered sex offender, Alcala managed to land a job with The Los Angeles Times as a typesetter in September 1977.

In September 1978, Alcala appeared as Bachelor No. 1 on a dating TV show that had men and women cheekily interview prospective dates, sight unseen. At the time he was a convicted child molester but the show did not run a background check. He was introduced as "a successful photographer, who got his start when his father found him in the darkroom at the age of 13, fully developed." When asked by Bradshaw, his prospective date, to describe what kind of meal he'd be, he answered, "I'm called 'The Banana', and I look really good ... Peel me."

Alcala often told women he was a fashion photographer who wanted to take photos for a contest. In the 1970s, he killed Cornelia Crilley, 23, and Ellen Hover, 23, both residents of New York City. Crilley was raped and strangled with her stockings in her apartment in June 1971. Hover disappeared on July 15, 1977, leaving behind a calendar that stated she was meeting with "John Berger." Her remains were discovered in New York's Westchester County in 1978.

Alcala was arrested in July 1979 for the abduction and murder of 12-year-old Robin Samsoe of Huntington Beach, California. He was convicted on these charges in 1980. Four years later this conviction was overturned as the jury had improperly been told about Alcala's criminal record. Another trial in 1986 resulted in a second guilty verdict, but in 2001 this was also overturned on a technicality.

Alcala pleaded guilty to these murders in 2012. He received a sentence of 25 to life, though it will only be served if California releases him from custody. In addition, he faced charges for assaulting and strangling four women in California in the late 1970s: 18-year-old Jill Barcomb, who was killed in November 1977, 27-year-old Georgia Wixted, 27, who was raped, beaten, and strangled in December 1978, 32-year-old Charlotte Lamb, who was killed in June 1978 and 21-year-old Jill Parenteau, who was killed in June 1979. Alcala opted to represent himself during the court proceedings. In February 2010 he was found guilty of all five murders. He was sentenced to death in March 2010.

In 2016, Alcala was charged with the 1977 killing of Christine Ruth Thornton in Wyoming, though prosecutors opted not to extradite him to stand trial. Authorities also believe he killed Pamela Lambson in the San Francisco Bay Area in the fall of 1977. However, DNA collected at that crime scene was too degraded to test, so he was not charged with the crime.

Following Alcala's arrest in July 1979, police found hundreds of his photographs in a Seattle storage locker. These images, some of which were explicit, may include other Alcala victims. In 2010 police shared many of these photos with the public in the hopes of identifying those in the pictures. Some people were alive and came forward. The photos aided in identifying Thornton as one of Alcala's victims. Some authorities believe he murdered around 50 people, others think he may have taken as many as 130 lives.

RANDY KRAFT

1945-

Birthplace

Long Beach

Zodiac Sign

Pisces

Modus Operandi

Raping

Torture

Strangulation

Confirmed Victims

16

Randy Kraft, in full Randy Steven Kraft, also known as the Scorecard Killer, was born on March 19, 1945, in Long Beach, California, but his family moved to Orange County when he was three years old.

Considered intelligent and scholarly (later testing with an IQ of 129), he graduated high school in 1963 and enrolled in Claremont Men's College, and joined the Reserve Officer Training Corps. For a while, he continued to remain conservative, demonstrating in favor of the Vietnam War and campaigning for Republican candidate Barry Goldwater for the 1964 election.

For some reasons, his political beliefs started changing the following year; he even got a job as a bartender at a gay bar. During his final year, there were rumors that he enjoyed bondage. According to a roommate, Kraft would disappear a few times a week and then return at strange hours. He also suffered from stomach pains and migraines and frequently took Valium to treat it.

During the 1970s and 1980s, the victims of Kraft were among the many dead bodies found near highways in California. While the investigators believed the murders to be the work of a single serial killer, who was dubbed "The Highway Killer", there were two other perpetrators, William Bonin and Patrick Kearney, besides Kraft, who was the last of the three to be caught. In all cases, the victims were males who suffered some kind of sexual abuse and torture before being killed.

Kraft's killings are believed to have started in 1971, the victim being Wayne Joseph Dukette, though Kraft was never convicted of his murder. He was first arrested on suspicion of murder when the severed head of one of his victims, Keith Crotwell, was found near the Long Beach Marina. Since he had been seen getting into a car revealed to be Kraft's, he was questioned as a suspect, but he claimed he let him ride along with him and then let him off at an all-night café. Kraft was released due to a lack of evidence.

He was caught for the last time, just after 1:00 a.m. on May 14, 1983, when the California Highway Patrol pulled him over for driving under the influence. When the officers looked into his car, they saw a man who appeared to be sleeping in the back seat. When they opened it, they found him to be dead, with obvious signs of foul play. The man was Terry Gambrel, a 25-year-old U.S. Marine officer and Kraft's final victim, and had been strangled with his own belt.

When a search warrant for the car was obtained and carried out, the police found tranquilizers and prescription drugs inside as well as an envelope containing 47 photographs of young men, most of them either dead or seemingly asleep, in pornographic poses. There was also a lot of blood on the passenger seat, even though Gambrel did not have any lacerations on his body.

When Kraft's home was searched as well, more evidence was found, including possessions of murder victims and Kraft's "score-card", on which he listed his victims by strange nicknames related to their locations or personal habits, such as "Deoderant", "New Year's Eve", and "Iowa". Kraft claimed the terms on the list referred to sexual encounters he had had and other mundane things.

A number of Randy's victims were military officers who were hitchhiking. After picking them up in his car, he would drug them and/or get them drunk; bind them; torture them by burning a car cigarette lighter against their face, chest, and genitals; sexually abuse them, and kill them in various ways, such as strangulation, asphyxiation, bludgeoning, or from a combination of torture and drugs. He would also castrate them, either as another form of torture or post-mortem, or mutilate and dismember them. He took photos of his victims while they were unconscious or even dead and would keep a record of his victims (hence his nickname) on a sheet of paper with nicknames for each victim written down on it. He would always dump the bodies near highways in southern California. Some of his confirmed and suspected victims were found with some object inserted into their rectums, most often a sock. The victims were also often found barefoot, sometimes fully clothed everywhere else; some suspect that Kraft did this because of a foot fetish. Kraft also bit his victims, usually on and/or around the genitals or the nipples.

In the end, Kraft was charged with 16 murders.

DOROTHEA PUENTE

1929-2011

Birthplace

Redlands

Zodiac Sign

Capricorn

Modus Operandi

Drugging

Burial

Confirmed Victims

3

Dorothea Puente, in full Dorothea Helen Puente (née Gray), also known as Death House Landlady, was born on January 9, 1929, in Redlands, California, the U.S, and died on March 27, 2011.

She had a traumatic upbringing; her parents were both alcoholics and her father repeatedly threatened to commit suicide in front of his children. Her father died of tuberculosis in 1937; her mother lost custody of her children in 1938 and died in a motorcycle accident by the end of the year. Puente and her siblings were subsequently sent to an orphanage, where she was sexually abused.

Gray's first marriage, at the age of sixteen, in 1945, was to a soldier named Fred McFaul, who had just returned from the

Pacific theater of World War II. Gray had two daughters between 1946 and 1948; she sent one child to live with relatives in Sacramento and placed the other for adoption. McFaul left her in late 1948 after she suffered a miscarriage. In the spring of 1948, Gray was arrested for purchasing women's accessories using forged checks in Riverside. She was charged and pled guilty to two counts of forgery, serving four months in jail and three years' probation. Six months after her release, she left Riverside.

In 1952, Gray married merchant seaman Axel Bren Johansson in San Francisco. She created a fake persona, calling herself "Teya Singoalla Neyaarda", and claiming to be a Muslim of Egyptian and Israeli descent. They had a turbulent marriage; Gray would take advantage of Johansson's frequent trips to sea by inviting men to their home and gambling away his money. In 1961, Johansson had Gray briefly committed to DeWitt State Hospital after a binge of drinking, lying, criminal behavior, and suicide attempts. While there, doctors diagnosed her as a pathological liar with an unstable personality. Gray and Johansson divorced in 1966.

Gray ran a boarding house located at 21st and F streets in

Sacramento. She established herself as a genuine resource to the community to aid alcoholics, homeless people, and mentally ill people by holding Alcoholics Anonymous meetings and assisting individuals to sign up to receive Social Security benefits.

She changed her public image to that of a respectable older matron by putting on vintage clothing, wearing large granny glasses, and letting her hair turn gray. She also established herself as a respected member of Sacramento's Hispanic community, funding charities, scholarships, and radio programs.

Between 1982 and 1989, Puente would take in the vulnerable and homeless – poisoning some of her guests before burying them on her property and cashing their social security checks. The disappearances of these so-called "shadow people" went unnoticed for years, until eventually a social worker Judy Moise reported a tenant missing. Suspicions first arose about Puente in 1988, after Judy, an outreach counselor with Volunteers of America, noticed 52-year-old Alvaro Montoya – someone she'd placed at Puente's house – had vanished. Alvaro had struggled with his mental health and been homeless for years, and Judy did not buy Puente's explanation that he had left for a holiday in Mexico with his brother – especially as she knew he did not speak to his family. Judy also questioned another of Puente's tenants, John Sharp, who told her she had been digging a lot of holes.

The police returned and searched the house, finding nothing, so they asked permission to dig up the garden. Finally, they found the body of 78-year-old Leona Carpenter, and the police realized what they thought was beef jerky was human flesh.

However, due to there being no evidence to link Puente to the body, Puente was allowed to leave and meet her nephew. Later, she managed to flee to Los Angeles, where she was found five days later when a man in a bar recognized her on TV. Meanwhile, another six bodies had been found in Puente's back garden, including those of 51-year-old Alberto Montoya, 64-year-old Dorothy Miller, 55-year-old Benjamin Fink, 62-year-old James Gallop, 64-year-old Vera Faye Martin, and 78-year-old Betty Palmer. She'd also been linked to another two previous deaths that were now seen as too similar to ignore. One of these was of a 61-year-old woman named Ruth Monroe, who Puente persuaded to move into her house in April

1982, when her husband died.

A prosecutor called over 130 witnesses to the stand. He stated that Puente used sleeping pills to drug her tenants, suffocated them, and then hired convicts to bury them in the yard. Dalmane, which is a drug used for insomnia, was found in all seven of the exhumed bodies. Her lawyers argued that she might be a thief, but not a murderer. The defense called several witnesses, who showed Puente had a generous and caring side to her. Witnesses, including her long-lost daughter, testified how Puente had helped them in their youth and guided them to successful careers.

Puente was convicted of three of the murders, although the jury could not agree on the other six. She was incarcerated at Central California Women's Facility (CCWF) in Chowchilla, California. For the rest of her life, she maintained her innocence, insisting that all of her boarders had died of "natural causes". Puente was said to be one of the most "cold and calculating female killers the country had ever seen".

Puente died in prison from natural causes in 2011.

PETER SUTCLIFFE

1946-2020

Birthplace
Bingley

Zodiac Sign
Gemini

Modus Operandi
Strangulation
Stabbing

Confirmed Victims
13

Peter Sutcliffe, also known as Peter William Coonan, was born on June 2, 1946, in Bingley, West Yorkshire, England, and died on November 13, 2020.

His father was well-liked and friendly, and so his parents hoped that he would grow up to be like him. Instead, Peter was shy, introverted, quiet, and preferred reading to playing sports. He was closer to his mother, whom his father suspected of having an affair. In secondary school, he was often bullied, driving him to truancy.

Leaving school at the age of 15, he spent two years at various jobs. Sutcliffe then got an engineering apprenticeship but dropped out after a few weeks. After a brief period working as a laborer at a factory, Peter took a job as a who was also a sex worker, in May. In April 1979, Sutcliffe killed Josephine Whittaker, a 19-year-old bank clerk. According to one police detective, "mass hysteria" ensued because more women felt threatened; Whittaker, who'd been killed while walking home, was seen as a "respectable" woman. Fears also heightened following the death of 20-year-old student Barbara Leach in September 1979. Sutcliffe took two more lives in 1980: civil servant Marguerite Walls, 47, in August and 20-year-old Jacqueline Hill, a student, in November.

Sutcliffe was arrested in the city of Sheffield on January 2, 1981. He was sitting in a car with a sex worker, Olivia Reivers when police spotted his fake license plates. After he was taken into custody, police discovered screwdrivers in Sutcliffe's car, which resulted in a search that uncovered a hammer and knife stashed near the scene of his arrest (he'd gotten a private moment by telling officers he needed to relieve himself). During his interrogation, Sutcliffe confessed to the crimes, saying, "It's all right, I know what you're leading up to. The Yorkshire Ripper. It's me. I killed all those women."

Sutcliffe was convicted in 1981 of murdering 13 women in Yorkshire and Manchester between 1975 and 1980. In these brutal crimes, victims were often battered with a hammer, as well as being stabbed and mutilated with a knife or sharpened screwdriver. At his 1981 trial, Sutcliffe was also found guilty of attacking seven other women in the 1975 to 1980 time period. These victims survived, though with lasting trauma and severe injuries.

Sutcliffe's trial began on May 4, 1981. Though he'd confessed to being the Yorkshire Ripper after his January arrest, in court he pleaded guilty to manslaughter but not guilty to murder, claiming diminished responsibility (akin to a plea of temporary insanity in the United States). Sutcliffe shared that he'd killed sex workers due to his belief that he was on a "divine mission."

In 1984, a diagnosis of paranoid schizophrenia saw Sutcliffe removed from prison and sent to Broadmoor Hospital, a secure psychiatric facility. While in custody, Sutcliffe applied for the right to parole, but a 2010 ruling said that he would never be released from prison. In 1997, an inmate stabbed Sutcliffe's eyes with a pen, and he subsequently lost vision in his left eye. He died at the age of 74 on November 13, 2020, in the University Hospital of North Durham, near the prison where he'd been serving his sentence.

CHIKATILO

1936-1994

Birthplace

Yablochnoye

Zodiac Sign

Libra

Modus Operandi

Stabbing

Torturing

Multilating

Confirmed Victims

52

Andrei Chikatilo, in full Andrei Romanovich Chikatilo, also known as Rostov Ripper, was born on October 16, 1936, in Yablochnoye, U.S.S.R. [now Ukraine], and died on February 14, 1994, in Moscow, Russia.

He grew up in the aftermath of the great Ukrainian famine of the 1930s, during which millions of people died and many resorted to cannibalism to survive.

During his childhood, he was told constantly by his mother that he had an older brother who had been kidnapped and eaten by neighbors. The story, which cannot be verified, apparently motivated Chikatilo to cannibalize some of his victims. Chikatilo was an avid reader with a particular interest in stories that described how German prisoners were tortured by their Soviet captors during World War II. After completing his military service, Chikatilo became a telephone engineer near Rostov-na-Donu, where he married in 1963. In 1971, he received a degree from Rostov Liberal Arts University and became a teacher. He was forced to resign his position, however, after some parents complained of sexual assaults by Chikatilo on their children.

His first known victim was killed on 22nd December 1978. The victim was 9-year-old Lena Zakotnova. It is believed that he lured her into an abandoned shed, where he attempted to rape her. While trying to stop the girl from struggling, Andrei Chikatilo slashed her with a knife, ejaculating whilst doing so.

There was an eyewitness that had seen him with the victim, shortly before her disappearance, but his wife provided him with an alibi so solid, that he managed to elude police attention. For the murder of his first victim, a 25-year-old, Alexsandr Kravchenko, with a previous rape conviction, was arrested. It is believed that his confession of killing the victim was done under duress. In 1984, Alexsandr Kravchenko was executed. On September 3, 1981, he struck his second victim. Larisa Tkachenko, 17 years old, became his victim. Chikatilo strangled, stabbed, and gagged her with earth and leaves to prevent her from crying out. He started following a pattern in choosing his victims. Mostly young runaways, not being missed by their families. He used to target them at train or bus stations, luring them into abandoned sheds or forest areas. He then proceeded to viciously attack them, rape them and mutilate them. Investigations showed that in some cases he ate the sexual organs of his victims, or removed body parts such as the tips of their noses or tongues. At the beginning of his killing spree, he used to damage the eyes of his victims, believing that the eyes hold an imprint of his face even after death.

During the year 1984, 15 more bodies were added to the count. By this time, police efforts intensified, most train and bus stations being under surveillance leading authorities to arrest Chikatilo for behaving suspiciously at a bus station. Although the briefcase he was carrying was found to contain a long knife and other suspicious instruments, police misidentified his blood type, which their tests showed did not match the type indicated by semen found at one of the crime scenes. Chikatilo was subsequently charged with theft of materials from a former employer and sentenced to one year in prison, though he was released after three months. After his release, Chikatilo resumed killing, and the subsequent police investigation, which included 24-hour surveillance of bus and train stations in one district, was intensive. On one occasion, he actually bit a nipple off of a young female victim and swallowed it, causing him to ejaculate. Sometimes, he stuffed his victims' mouths with mud and leaves to muffle their screams (similar to fellow serial killer Arthur Shawcross). He often cannibalized their remains and sometimes drank their blood.

In 1990, he was identified as the chief suspect in the crimes and arrested; at the time of his arrest, he was carrying a briefcase containing items similar to those in his possession when he was detained six years earlier. While in custody, Chikatilo confessed, and later he was transported to various crime scenes to demonstrate his methods to the police.

Chikatilo confessed to fifty-six murders and was tried for fifty-three of them in April 1992. He was convicted and sentenced to death for fifty-two of these murders in October 1992, although the Supreme Court of Russia ruled in 1993 that insufficient evidence existed to prove his guilt in nine of those killings. Chikatilo was executed by gunshot in February 1994.

DEAN CORLL

1939–1973

Birthplace
Fort Wayne

Zodiac Sign
Capricorn

Modus Operandi
Raping
Strangulation
Shooting

Suspected Victims
28–76+

Dean Corll, in full Dean Arnold Corll, was born on December 24, 1939, in Fort Wayne, Indiana, the U.S. and died on August 8, 1973, in Pasadena, Texas.

After the separation of his parents, Corll along with his mother shifted base to Memphis, Tennessee. As a child, he was shy. He rarely socialized with children but was fond of them. Corll suffered from an undiagnosed rheumatic fever that led to a heart murmur.

Corll's mother remarried Jack West in 1955. Together they started a small family candy company named 'Pecan Prince'. Young Corll together with his brother operated the candy-making machine and packed the product while his father sold them on his sales route.

In 1962, Corll returned to Houston to help in his family's candy business. The following year, after his parents divorced, his mother started a new candy business, Corll Candy Company, of which Corll served as the vice-president. In 1964, Corll was drafted into the US Army. However, disliking the same, he requested an early acquittal which he was granted in June 1965. It was during his time in the army that Corll first realized that he was homosexual.

Following his honorable discharge from the army, Corll returned to Houston and resumed his position as vice-president. During that time, Corll earned the nickname the Candy Man and the Pied Piper for giving free candies to local children. He befriended David Brooks, his accomplice in the murders. What turned Dean Corll into a murderer and sexual assaulter is unknown but by 1970, he had turned himself into one.

His first ever victim was an 18-year-old freshman Jeffrey Konen whom he caught on September 25, 1970, by offering him a drive. Konen was strapped to a plywood torture board and sexually assaulted. After Konen, Corll did not stop his brutal assault, his next target being James Glass and Danny Yates.

He picked the boys from the neighborhood of Houston Heights and lured them into his car. He then sexually assaulted them and buried them in the boat shed. His friend and accomplice, David Brooks helped him in the process.

Corll next picked up Donald and Jerry Waldrop, the brother duo, and took them to an apartment on Mangum Road. He then raped, tortured, strangled, and subsequently buried them in the boat shed. By May 1971, Corll abducted and killed three more victims (Radell Harvey, David Hilligiest, and Gregory Malley Winkle). Between August and September 1971, Corll changed his address twice and abducted three more victims. The trio met with the same fate as the other boys. During the winter of 1971, Henley was lured to Corll's house as an intended victim by David Brooks. However, instead of victimizing the boy, Corll lured him to a deal –$200 for every boy that Henley managed to get to Corll's apartment. Corll informed Henley that the boys were used for the white slavery ring operating from Dallas.

Henley accepted the offer and started bringing the boys to Corll's house. His first-ever 'client-victim' was a boy named Willard Branch from Houston Heights in February 1972. A month later, he lured Frank Aguirre to Corll's apartment.

It was during this time that Henley first got acquainted with Corll's real intention. Despite knowing the fact that Corll used the boys for his lust and later murdered them, Henley did not move back and instead further helped Brooks and Corll in this vicious act. Corll kept rotating his residential address and did not stay at one apartment for long. With the assistance from Brooks and Henley, he targeted almost 10 teenage boys between February and November 1972, five of whom were buried at High Island Beach and the rest five in his boat shed.

After a period of inactivity from February to June 1973, Corll returned to the malicious violence, this time the brutality being more severe. Furthermore, the acceleration in the frequency of killings also increased severely. In just two weeks, he victimized two teenage boys and buried them at Lake Sam Rayburn. His lustful vengeance and his merciless bloodshed became all the more ruthless.

In July 1973, Henley became the sole procurer of victims for Corll as his accomplice David Brooks got married off. He brought Corll three more victims who met with the same tragic fate. Corll killed his last victim on August 3, 1973. The victim was a 13-year-old boy from South Houston named James

Dreymala. Dreymala was abducted by Brooks and driven to Corll's home where he was tied to Corll's torture board, raped, tortured, and strangled with a cord before being buried in the boat shed.

On August 7, 1973, Henley sweet-talked a teenage boy, Timothy Cordell Kerley as Corll's next victim. After a round of drug doses, Henley and Kerley went out for some fresh air. Meanwhile, they hit upon a girl Rhonda Williams who accompanied them to Corll's residence. The next day, after tying Kerley and Williams on the opposite side of the torture bed, he was about to rape them when Henley took hold of Corll's gun and fired him to death.

After he shot Corll, Henley released Kerley and Williams from the torture board. They called the Pasadena Police who seized the weapon, the .22 caliber gun and took them to the patrol car where Henley was questioned. He admitted to serving as an assistant to Corll who raped and murdered teenage boys. Henley admitted to abducting young boys, all of whom died in the process. He even agreed to accompany police in the search of the victim's bodies. David Brooks, who had earlier denied being directly involved in the acts, was later convicted after

after Henley passed a statement against him. Henley stated that except for only three abductions and murders Brooks had been directly involved in all of the rest.

By August 13, 1973, Henley and Brooks assisted police in their search of 27 victims' bodies. Later known as the Houston Mass Murder, Corll is said to have killed a minimum of 28 victims, the worst ever macabre record in American history.

Corll's victims were typically lured with an offer of a party or a lift to one of the various addresses he resided in between 1970 and 1973. They would then be restrained either by force or deception, and each was killed either by strangulation or shooting with a .22 caliber pistol. Corll and his accomplices buried 17 of their victims in a rented boat shed; four other victims were buried in woodland near Lake Sam Rayburn; one victim was buried on a beach in Jefferson County; and at least six victims were buried on a beach on the Bolivar Peninsula. Brooks and Henley confessed to assisting Corll in several abductions and murders; both were sentenced to life imprisonment at their subsequent trials.

DAVID RAY

1939-2002

Birthplace
Belen

Zodiac Sign
Taurus

Modus Operandi
Kidnapping
Drugging
Torturing

Suspected Victims
60

David Parker Ray, also known as the Toy-Box Killer, was born on November 6, 1939, in Belen, New Mexico, the U.S. and died on May 28, 2002.

His parents were Cecil and Nettie Ray. Due to their poor financial condition, the family lived with his mother's parents on a small ranch where David grew up with his sister Peggy. His father was a drunkard who often quarreled with and lashed out at his mother.

David's father often supplied him with magazines that depicted sadomasochistic pornography. As he was shy and socially awkward, he was bullied by his peers. This led to his secret fascination with sadomasochism. After he completed his high school education, he worked as an auto mechanic. He also worked in the army, from where he eventually received an honorable discharge. David Parker Ray had been married and divorced four times. He had children, including a daughter named Jesse Ray.

It is believed that David Ray started his killing spree somewhere in the mid-1950s. He is known to have had multiple accomplices including some of the women he was dating. He is believed to have terrorized and killed many women using items, such as whips, straps, sex toys, etc. It is also said that he prefered to let his victims see how he employed different techniques and methods for inflicting pain on them.

David Parker Ray's crimes eventually came to an end in March 1999, when he was 59. On March 19th, he approached a 22-year-old woman named Cynthia Vigil in a parking lot, pretending to be a cop. He told her she was under arrest for sex work. He put her in the back of his car, and brought her to his soundproof trailer, which he called his 'Toy Box'. He then chained her to a table, and over the next three days, he raped and tortured her. He was also helped by his girlfriend Cindy Hendy. They used whips, medical instruments, electronic shocks, as well as sexual instruments to torture Cynthia Vigil. Ray also played a cassette tape recording with details of what she would go through. He also told her to refer to them as master and mistress. He explained the details of how he would rape and torture her as well. He sexually assaulted and tortured her for three days. On the third day, when Ray was at work, his girlfriend left the keys to Vigil's restraints on a table by mistake, after which she left the room.

When Vigil tried to escape, Hendy noticed it and broke a lamp on her head. Despite this, Vigil managed to unlock her chains and used an icepick to stab Hendy in the neck. After Hendy fell to the floor, Vigil managed to escape. Vigil ran down the road wearing an iron slave collar and padlocked chains till a homeowner took her in. The police were called and Parker and his accomplices were captured.

When the news about the arrest spread, another victim named Angelica Montano came forward and said that she had also been victimized by Parker. Though she had reported to the police, there had been no follow-up in the case. Many other women who had been kidnapped from Raymond's Lounge and tortured also came forward, and it was found that the manager of Raymond's Lounge was also an accomplice. A few members of the law enforcement were also found to be accomplices.

The FBI sent numerous agents to investigate Ray's property and surroundings. However, no identifiable human remains could be found through the police believed that he had murdered numerous people.

During the trial, the prosecution brought forward two identified victims, Cynthia Vigil and Kelli Garrett, as well as the mother of a deceased victim. The women testified against Ray and described the horrible tortures that they had to go through.

After being convicted of numerous offenses, Ray was sentenced to 224 years in prison. His girlfriend Hendy, who had testified against Ray, also received a 36-year sentence for her role in the crimes. His daughter Jesse Ray was also sentenced to two and a half years in prison for her involvement in the crimes. She also received an additional five years to be served on probation.

In May 2002, Ray was taken to the Lea County Correctional Facility in Hobbs, New Mexico to be questioned. However, he died of a heart attack on 28 May before the interrogation could take place.

SERIAL KILLERS' QUOTES

"We serial killers are your sons, we are your husbands, we are everywhere. And there will be more of your children dead tomorrow"

— TED BUNDY

"I don't think anybody doubts whether I've done some bad things. The question is: what, of course, and how...and most importantly, why?"

— TED BUNDY

"Guilt. It's this mechanism we use to control people. It's an illusion. It's a kind of social control mechanism and it's very unhealthy. It does terrible things to the body."

— TED BUNDY

"I don't want to die. I'm not going to kid you. I deserve the most extreme punishment society has...I think society deserves to be protected from me and others like me."

— TED BUNDY

"The ultimate possession was, in fact, the taking of the life. And then...the physical possession of the remains."

— TED BUNDY

"When I see a pretty girl walking down the street, I think two things. One party wants to be real nice and sweet, and the other part wonders what her head would look like on a stick"

- EG GEIN

"One side of me says, I'd like to talk to her, date her. The other side of me says, I wonder what her head would look like on a stick?"

- EDMUND KEMPER

"It was an urge. . . . . A strong urge, and the longer I let it go the stronger it got, to where I was taking risks to go out and kill people-risks that normally, according to my little rules of operation, I wouldn't take because they could lead to arrest."

- EDMUND KEMPER

"I certainly wanted for my mother a nice, quiet easy death like everyone else wants."

- EDMUND KEMPER

"With a girl, there's a lot left in the girl's body without a head. Of course, the personality is gone."

- EDMUND KEMPER

"The first good-looking girl I see tonight is going to die."

– EDMUND KEMPER

"I had thought of annihilating the entire block that I lived on."

– EDMUND KEMPER

"I remember there was actually a sexual thrill . . . you hear that little pop and pull their heads of and hold their heads up by the hair. Whipping their heads off, their body sitting there. That'd get me off."

– EDMUND KEMPER

"Even psychopaths have emotions. Then again, maybe not."

– RICHARD RAMIREZ

"Serial killers do, on a small scale, what governments do on a large one. They are products of our times and these are bloodthirsty times."

– RICHARD RAMIREZ

"We've all got the power in our hands to kill, but most people are afraid to use it."

– RICHARD RAMIREZ

"In the end, we all die, and nothing really matters."

— RICHARD RAMIREZ

"We are all evil in some form or another, are we not?"

— RICHARD RAMIREZ

"One time I told this lady to give me all her money, she said no. So I cut her and pulled her eyes out. I would do someone in and then take a camera and set the timer so I could sit them up next to me and take our picture together."

— RICHARD RAMIREZ

"I gave up love and happiness a long time ago."

— RICHARD RAMIREZ

"I am beyond your experience. I am beyond good and evil, legions of the night – night breed – repeat not the errors of the Night Stalker and show no mercy."

— RICHARD RAMIREZ

"I killed so many women I have a hard time keeping them straight."

— GARY RIDGWAY

"I always wondered what it would be like to kill someone."

— GARY RIDGWAY

"I'm a murderer, not a rapist."

— GARY RIDGWAY

"I also picked prostitutes as victims because they were easy to pick up, without being noticed. I knew they would not be reported missing right away, and might never be reported missing."

— GARY RIDGWAY

"I don't care if I live or die. Go ahead and kill me."

— JEFFREY DAHMER

"I had a box in my bedroom closet and it contained the mummified head and genitals of a young man I met in one of the bars down in Milwaukee"

— JEFFREY DAHMER

"Looking back on my life, I know I have made others suffer as much as I have suffered."

— JEFFREY DAHMER

"For what I did I should be dead."

— JEFFREY DAHMER

"It's hard for me to believe that a human being could have done what I've done, but I know I did it."

— JEFFREY DAHMER

"That was the least satisfactory part. I didn't enjoy doing that. That's why I tried to create living zombies with uric acid in the drill to the head, but it never worked."

— JEFFREY DAHMER

"Yes, I always had that sense it was wrong. I don't think anybody can kill somebody and think that it's right."

— JEFFREY DAHMER

"I don't remember killing anyone, I could have done it without knowing it. I am not sure if I did it."

— JOHN WAYNE GACY

"The dead won't bother you, it's the living you have to worry about."

— JOHN WAYNE GACY

"A clown can get away with murder."

- JOHN WAYNE GACY

"I should never have been convicted of anything more serious than running a cemetery without a license."

- JOHN WAYNE GACY

"The idea that I'm a homosexual thrill killer, that I stroll down the streets and stalk young boys and slaughter them... Hell, if you could see my schedule, my work schedule, you knew damn well that I was never out there."

- JOHN WAYNE GACY

"I am a serial killer. I would kill again."

- AILEEN WUORNOS

"I wanted to clear all the lies and let the truth come out. I have hate crawling through my system."

- AILEEN WUORNOS

"They say it's the number of people I killed, I say it's the principle."

- AILEEN WUORNOS

"There is no point in sparing me. It's a waste of taxpayers' money."

- AILEEN WUORNOS

"I robbed them, and I killed them as cold as ice, and I would do it again, and I know I would kill another person because I've hated humans for a long time."

- AILEEN WUORNOS

"To me, this world is nothing but evil, and my own evil just happened to come out cause of the circumstances of what I was doing."

- AILEEN WUORNOS

"When this monster entered my brain, I will never know, but it is here to stay. How does one cure himself? I can't stop it, the monster goes on, and hurts me as well as society. Maybe you can stop him. I can't."

- DENNIS RADER

"I actually think I may be possessed with demons, I was dropped on my head as a kid."

- DENNIS RADER

"I have several children who I'm turning into killers. Wait till they grow up."

- DAVID BERKOWITZ

"The people and the news media used to call me 'The Son of Sam,' but God has given me a new name, 'The Son of Hope,' because now my life is about hope."

- DAVID BERKOWITZ

"A 'possessed' dog in the neighborhood won't let me stop killing until he gets his fill of blood."

- DAVID BERKOWITZ

"I didn't want to hurt them, I only wanted to kill them."

- DAVID BERKOWITZ

"I always had a fetish for murder and death."

- DAVID BERKOWITZ

"I want to report a murder, no, a double murder. They are two miles north of Park Headquarters. They were in a white Volkswagen Karmann Ghia. I'm the one that did it."

- THE ZODIAC KILLER

"The police shall never catch me, because I have been too clever for them."

— THE ZODIAC KILLER

"I like killing people because it is so much fun. It is more fun than killing wild game in the forest because man is the most dangerous animal of all."

— THE ZODIAC KILLER

"I'm Jack the Ripper. I love women. I'm Jack the Ripper. I caused terror throughout London-"

— JACK THE RIPPER

"Ninety years ago I was a freak. Today I'm an amateur."

— JACK THE RIPPER

"One day men will look back and say I gave birth to the twentieth century."

— JACK THE RIPPER

"The women I killed were filth – bastard prostitutes who were littering the streets. I was just cleaning up the place a bit."

— PETER SUTCLIFFE

"Killing prostitutes had become an obsession with me. I could not stop myself. It was like a drug."

- PETER SUTCLIFFE

"I thought 'God, what have I done?'... I realized I would be in serious trouble. I thought the best way out of the mess was to make sure she could not tell anybody."

- PETER SUTCLIFFE

"When I used my knife, it brought psychological relief. I know I have to be destroyed. I was a mistake of nature."

- ANDREI CHIKATILO

"I am a mistake of nature, a mad beast."

- ANDREI CHIKATILO

"What I did was not for sexual pleasure. Rather it brought me some peace of mind."

- ANDREI CHIKATILO

"You're going to be kept here naked and chained down. I'm going to use you for a sex slave."

- DAVID RAY

QUIZ TIME

Match Each Serial Killer With His/Her Alias

1.	Ted Bundy	a.	The Butcher of Plainfield
2.	Ed Gein	b.	The Co-Ed Killer
3.	Ed Kemper	c.	The Green River Killer
4.	Richard Ramirez	d.	The Night Stalker
5.	Gary Ridgway	e.	Pogo the Clown
6.	Harold Shipman	f.	The Milwaukee Cannibal
7.	Jeffrey Dahmer	g.	Dr. Death
8.	John Wayne Gacy	h.	The Toy-Box Killer
9.	Aileen Wuornos	i.	The Scorecard Killer
10.	Dennis Rader	j.	The Death House Landlady
11.	David Berkowitz	k.	The Dating Game Killer
12.	Rodney Alcala	l.	The BTK Killer
13.	Randy Kraft	m.	Son of Sam
14.	Dorothea Puente	n.	The Yorkshire Ripper
15.	Peter Sutcliffe	o.	The Butcher of Rostov
16.	Andrei Chikatilo	p.	The Damsel of Death
17.	David Ray	q.	The Lady Killer

....

....

....

Circle the Correct Answer

1. What was the make and model of Ted Bundy's infamous vehicle?

a. Volkswagen Beetle

b. Chevrolet Corvette

c. Ford Mustang

d. Mercedes-Benz

2. How many times did Ted Bundy escape prison?

a. Once

b. Twice

c. Three Times

d. Four Times

3. What was Eddie Gein's mother's name?

a. Augusta

b. Audrey

c. Agatha

d. Adelle

4. How many people did Eddie admit to killing?

a. 7

b. 3

c. 2

d. 5

5. Edmund was a giant of a man, and towered over friends and victims alike. How tall was he?

a. 7' 2"

b. 7' 5"

c. 6' 5"

d. 6' 9"

6. How was Edmund caught?

a. Police tracked him to his dead mother.

b. He turned himself in.

c. Fingerprints on the wrapping of a victim's body.

d. Pulled over by police with a victim in his car.

7. Which of these serial killers ate his victims?

a. Ted Bundy

b. Charles Manson

c. John Wayne Gacy

d. Jeffrey Dahmer

8. When did Richard Ramirez die?

a. 2012

b. 2013

c. 2014

d. 2015

9. What does MO in a serial killer's MO stand for?

a. Method of operation

b. Murder operation

c. Modus operandi

d. Means of operation

10. Where was Gary Ridgway born?

a. Salt Lake City, Utah

b. El Paso, Texas

c. Pittsburg, Kansas

d. Redlands, California

11. When did Shipman receive a medical degree from Leeds Uni?

a. 1970

b. 1971

c. 1972

d. 1973

12. At Harold Shipman's trial in 2000, how many counts of murder were brought against him?

a. 15

b. 17

c. 16

d. 18

13. During questioning by detectives, who did Richard Ramirez claim he idolized?

a. Jack The Ripper

b. Ted Bundy

c. John Wayne Gacy

d. The Hillside Stranglers

14. How did Jeffrey Dahmer kill the majority of his victims?

a. He poisoned them

b. He stabbed them

c. He strangled them

d. He shot them

15. In what year did John Wayne Gacy kill his first victim?

a. 1978

b. 1970

c. 1972

d. 1976

16. How was John Wayne Gacy executed?

a. Gassing

b. Lethal injection

c. Electric chair

d. Firing squad

17. What is Aileen's middle name?

a. Carol

b. Shawna

c. Marie

d. Jane

18. What did Aileen get as her last meal?

a. Bread and butter

b. Jellybeans

c. Coffee

d. French Fries

19. What does BTK stand for?

a. Buying Time to Kill

b. Be The Killer

c. Bind, Torture, Kill

d. Been known To Kill

20. Whose DNA was used to link Dennis Rader to the BTK killings?

a. DNA was not used in identifying BTK

b. His daughter's

c. His brother's

d. A victim's

21. What weapon did Son of Sam use?

a. Knife

b. Shotgun

c. Rifle

d. Handgun

22. How many years was Berkowitz sentenced to prison?

a. 365

b. 150

c. 395

d. 235

23. Where did Jack The Ripper crimes take place?

a. Cardiff

b. Edinburgh

c. London

d. Liverpool

24. How many known murders was Jack The Ripper credited with?

a. 5

b. 12

c. 25

d. 8

25. What is NOT the Zodiac Killer's pattern?

a. Targeting teenage couples

b. Shooting or stabbing the victims

c. Using a simple handgun

d. Cannibalism

26. Why was Alcala discharged from the military?

a. He raped a college student

b. He was diagnosed with antisocial personality disorder

c. He was lazy

d. He shared marijuana with other soldiers

27. How old was the Dating Game Killer when he died?

a. 76

b. 77

c. 78

d. 79

28. What was Randy Kraft's occupation when he worked at the gay bar?

a. Bartender

b. Waiter

c. Manager

d. Cashier

29. What was Dorothea Puente's zodiac sign?

a. Aries

b. Gemini

c. Capricorn

d. Cancer

30. Where was Dorothea Puente's boarding house?

a. Oakland

b. Sacramento

c. Mojave

d. Ridgecrest

31. What did Sutcliffe claim was the motive for the killings?

a. A hatred of women

b. Frustration at his own impotence

c. Revenge for abuse he had suffered as a child

d. The word of God

32. For how many murders was The Yorkshire Ripper convicted at his trial?

a. 20

b. 13

c. 15

d. 16

33. What is Andrei Chikatilo's nationality?

a. Ukrainian

b. American

c. Thai

d. Japanese

34. What kind of company did Dean Corll run?

a. Fruits

b. Candies

c. Women Underwear

d. Pets

35. Who was Cindy Hendy to David Ray?

a. Sister

b. Mother

c. Girlfriend

d. Victim

36. How are serial killers different from mass murderers?

a. Serial killers are more skilled

b. Serial killers let time pass between murders

c. Serial killers murder all their victims in a short amount of time

d. Serial killers killed more than 3

ANSWER KEYS

Match Each Serial Killer With His/Her Alias

1. q
2. a
3. b
4. d
5. c
6. g
7. f
8. e
9. p
10. l
11. m
12. k
13. i
14. j
15. n
16. o
17. h

Circle the Correct Answer

1.	a	19.	c
2.	b	20.	b
3.	a	21.	d
4.	c	22.	a
5.	d	23.	c
6.	b	24.	a
7.	d	25.	a
8.	b	26.	b
9.	c	27.	b
10.	a	28.	a
11.	a	29.	c
12.	a	30.	b
13.	d	31.	d
14.	c	32.	b
15.	c	33.	a
16.	b	34.	b
17.	a	35.	c
18.	c	36.	b

Printed in Great Britain
by Amazon

13570229R00068